PEÑA on PEÑA

AMADO PEÑA

amado maurilio peña Jr

WRS PUBLISHING

A Division of WRS Group, Inc.
Waco, Texas

First published in the United States of America in 1995 by WRS Publishing, A division of WRS Group, Inc., 701 N. New Road, Waco, Texas 76701. Book design by Kenneth Turbeville. Jacket design by Joe James.

Printed in Hong Kong

10 9 8 7 6 5 4 3 2 1

Library of Congress Cataloging-in-Publication Data
Peña, Amado Maurilio, 1943-
    Peña on Peña / Amado Peña.
       p.   cm.
    ISBN 1-56796-061-8 : $29.95
    1. Peña, Amado Maurilio, 1943- --Catalogs. 2. Mestizos-
  -Southwest, New--Portraits--Catalogs. 3. Indians of North America-
  -Southwest, New--Mixed descent--Portraits--Catalogs. I. Title.
N6537.P36A4   1995
760'.092--dc20   94-26331
                          CIP

DEDICATION

To Reuben Rose (1920-1994)
        thanks for a lifetime of
        friendship and for making me
        a better human being

To J.B.
        thanks for your support

To my father and mother
        amado y maria for their love

To my sister
        irene for all her prayers

To all mestizo people in this world —

Table of Contents

Amado Peña

Monument Valley, Spider Rock, Enchanted Mesa—these are
names that evoke an aura of mystery and hint at the birth of legends.
These sites are part of an enduring, rugged landscape that speaks of the
ancient heritage of a region now known as Arizona and New Mexico. This land,
the people who live there, and their native crafts are threads in a rich cultural
tapestry that is the inspiration for the works of Amado Maurilio Peña, Jr.

Growing up in the Lower Rio Grande Valley, Amado Peña, a mestizo of Spanish and Indian
ancestry, never dreamed that one day his career and his life would be linked by the waters which
flow from the Upper Rio Grande in New Mexico to the arid region of his hometown in Laredo, Texas.
Today, Amado's art is a superb blending of the landscapes and people of both regions. His paintings celebrate the strength of
a people who meet the harsh realities of life in an uncompromising land.

An appreciation of Mexican society and the values that went with it—close identification with the land, strong family
ties, and a powerful respect for elders—dominated Amado's upbringing.

Amado grew up in the streets of Laredo. His father was a fireman, his mother was a homemaker and seamstress, and his
sister Irene became a schoolteacher. He always had a deep respect for his family, for his roots. His folks have lived in the
same house since he was thirteen. As a kid, he stayed out of trouble and played a lot of football. "When I see `Happy Days,'"
he said, "it's like my youth."

No one in his family nor in Laredo turned him on to art. "I don't really understand what made me do what I did," he said.
There were no galleries, no museums, and very little art education in the public schools. He started drawing in the fourth
grade and never quit. War and cowboy comic books provided his first sketching lessons. When he attended Texas A&I in
Kingsville, all he wanted was a teaching degree. He took what studio classes were offered and spent additional hours ex-
ploring other mediums. After college, Amado taught in high school and set up a studio on the side. His work in those days

was academic: still lifes, color experimentation, and technical problem-solving.

In 1970, when he returned to Texas A&I for a master's degree in art education, Amado's art first began to reflect his appreciation for his Mexican-Mestizo roots. The Chicano Movement was in full swing, and through his art, Amado participated in the cause. During that period, 1970–1975, his art drew direct attention to the farmworkers' plight in south Texas and repudiated social deprivation and political inequities which Chicanos had encountered in the Southwest. Amado accepted a job as an art teacher in Crystal City in 1971, where he recognized that through his art he could successfully convey the political issues articulated by the community. He sought to lift the spirit of the community by giving the youth something in which they could take pride. He felt an understanding of Mexican history, especially of the Mexican Revolution, would give the community a sense of pride since, in that struggle, the "underdogs" had succeeded against great odds.

Photo credit: Harvey Morgan

"The two images that I used more at the time were Villa and Zapata," Amado remembers, "I used those images over and over, making different statements with them." The hard-riding Francisco Villa and the Indian peasant, Emiliano Zapata, represented cultural heroes to Amado and the Chicanos of the 1960s. In the Villa, Zapata, and also Che Guevara images, Amado's creativity and dynamic symbolism of marching farmworkers, bleeding lettuce, power to the people, and *carnales* killed by the police placed him among the foremost artistic spokesmen for the Chicano Movement. His art was fierce, revolutionary, and beautiful.

Then, abruptly, Amado quit painting. He had moved to Austin in 1973 to teach, and the demands for his protest art grew. But in 1975 two of his students were killed in a violent clash during a protest march in Denver and, traumatized by the brutalities of the political struggle, he made a complete break from his art.

For a while he just let things percolate, seeking new directions, equanimity. The following year he reemerged in a more gentle mode—so much bright color, traditional serene patterns of Southwest design, an intricate peacefulness of family and community togetherness. Amado refers to the period as the era he painted "primitives": small watercolors painted quickly and in large quantities, often sold in package form. Still, many of these watercolors are detailed and introspective statements about the people in Amado's life. While these works brought him minimal profits, painting again gave him a new sense of fulfillment.

Amado's travels to New Mexico's Upper Rio Grande Valley in the late 1970s came as a result of an invitation from educator/artist Ruben Rose. These travels introduced him to the Native American images and thus established new personal influences. Although the attachment to the region came naturally, his study of the old traditions and cultures continued. Aided by long conversations and visits with a fellow artist, Encarnacion Peña, and a deep, inspirational friendship with the immensely creative potter, Lucy Lewis, Amado's creative energies took a new direction. The mystique of the peoples of the Southwest immediately became a part of his painterly charm. At the same time, he gained an appreciation of the artistic works of Georgia O'Keeffe and T.C. Cannon.

This third period—Amado's contemporary art—defies simple characterization. It may be called Southwestern Mestizo. And, while the figures are mestizos, by Amado's own definition they are a part also of American Indian culture, although not holistically *the* American Indian. The wide arc extending from the hats of his male figures encompasses space, time, and ideals. The colorful serapes of Indian-Mestizo men and women and the physical features tell us that these images are of indigenous America. These subjects are, Amado tells us, "my people, the people around me."

Amado decided to leave teaching after sixteen years. "I was going to be a gypsy and do arts and crafts shows," he said. He traveled all over the Southwest to art fairs, where he set up booths and hawked his wares for whatever the market would bear. The hustle was fatiguing, but he stuck to it, and things changed: he was discovered. People bought, galleries called, and he sold and sold and sold.

Amado could barely keep up with the demand. He hired an assistant, and then another. He spent fourteen hours at a time in the studio, and still there wasn't enough time. Amado had touched a chord, learned to reach out to the masses, and had broken through. He quit teaching school and sold his paintings on the sidewalk.

Amado can't even guess the number of works he has created. "Thousands," he offers—hand-pulled lithographs and serigraphs, etchings, monotypes, and mixed-media originals. The reproduction venues have been just as numerous: prints, posters, T-shirts, tiles, cups, and on and on. His works are collected and displayed worldwide. To get control of his quickly expanding empire, Amado established El Taller, Inc. ("The Workshop") to manage the business end of his artistry. Under the namesake, he opened four galleries—two in Austin, the others in Taos and Santa Fe, New Mexico. He learned every aspect of the art business, including production and printing, negotiating with galleries, and publicizing events. But the demands became distracting and, in an effort to simplify his life and get back to basics and to people, he sold the galleries.

Amado now divides his time between two studios, one in Austin and another near Santa Fe, where he lives on a working ranch. He travels to one-man shows and art festivals across the country.

The people of Amado's art live and work surrounded by canyons, mesas, churches, and kivas. Like most masters, he transforms ordinary subjects into exotic magic. His women are powerful statements of pride and elegance. His pueblos and mesas are implacable and powerful, but his people mirror that strength and are its match. Amado's palette derives from nature, too. Air and water, fire and earth are its primary elements, showing men and women at peace with their surroundings. Using strong design elements and carefully selected color contrasts, Amado shows us in his art how these people respond to their environment, merge with it, and then dominate the land around them.

Amado Maurilio Peña, Jr., seeks to tell the story of a dignified people who inhabit a magisterial land. He understands that they are the survivors of frontier wars, floods, dust storms, and economic hard times, and he is fascinated by their endurance. In documenting their lives, he captures the essence of their existence. Like Georgia O'Keeffe, he is a master of his genre: opening windows for us to observe and appreciate great wonders.

La Portadora de Agua

Work is one of life's most beautiful experiences.
The Water Bearer is a portrait of a woman showing the
beauty of her work. She is represented as an elegant individual.
She carries water in her olla. The olla is a functional, yet artistic,
instrument constructed from clay, from the earth. It is a symbol of life
itself. I have shown the water being carried by the woman to emphasize her
strength. It is her strength that holds our family together. ✿

La Portadora de Agua – 18" x 24" Serigraph, 1980

CHRISTMAS IN SANTA FE

This celebration of Christmas captures the festive reenactments of Mary and Joseph looking for lodging and the wise men bearing gifts. These figures from the past are linked to the present as they are joined by children lighting the way and adults bearing gifts. The past and the present bring unity to make it whole. The recurring circle here and in other images represents life's cycle. No matter how far we go, we still come back to our beginnings. ✺

CHRISTMAS IN SANTE FE – 30" x 40" MIXED MEDIA PAINTING, 1980

SOUTHWEST SPIRIT

The circle of life is represented by the symbolic arch extending from the man's hat. This is a family unit, which I consider to be the spirit and soul of our Southwest culture. The man, like a giant tree, is the protector. The children represent the seeds, and the woman is the nurturer. While the man is larger in initial perspective, no one character is more important than the other. In the old tradition, the man is the protector and provider, while the woman is the strength that holds the family core together. ✺

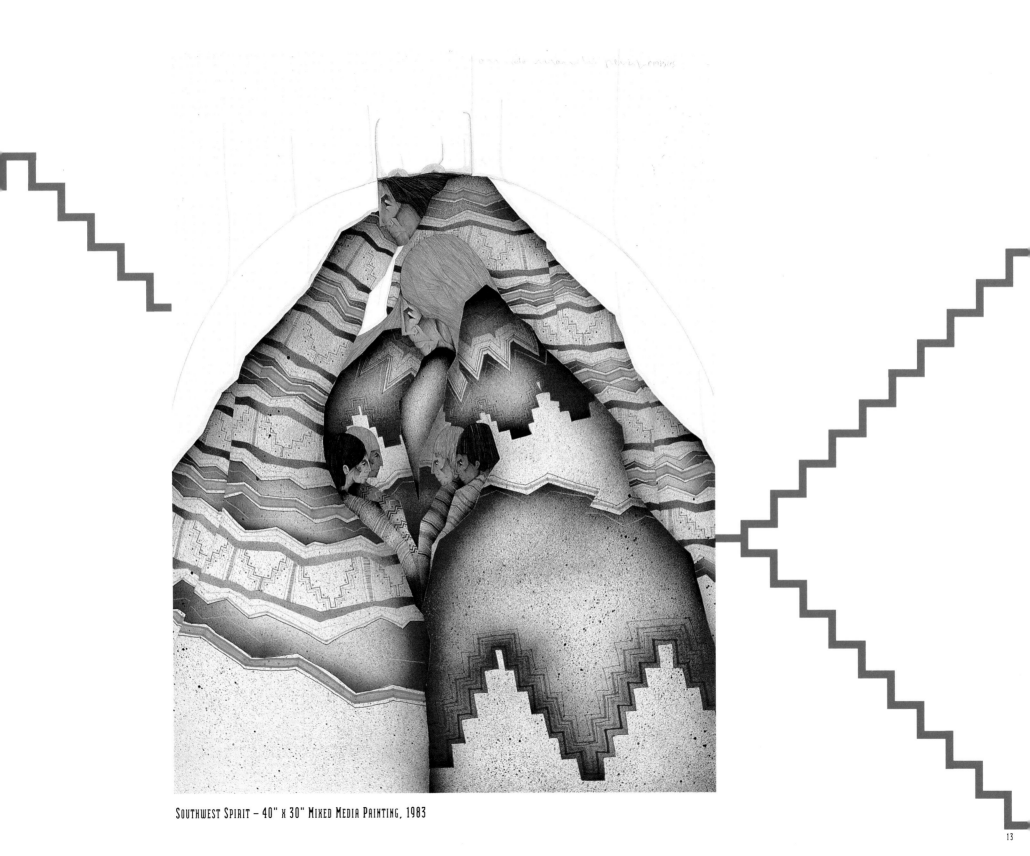

Southwest Spirit — 40" x 30" Mixed Media Painting, 1983

PARA LOS NINOS

For the Children is a painting dedicated to children.
It is a depiction of birth symbolized by children in the
womb. The circle extending from the parents' faces represents
the unity of life. The winds blowing in all directions in the sky
symbolize the spreading of the seeds of life. It is through our children
that our culture continues. ✸

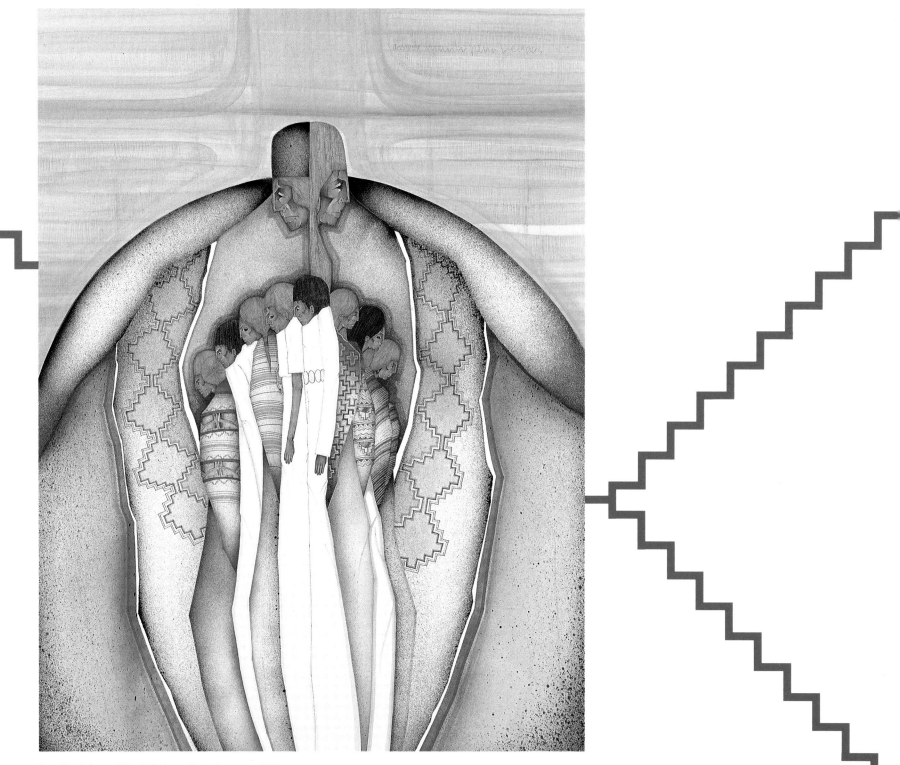

Para Los Niños — 32" x 24" Mixed Media Painting, 1983

DOS Y EL PUEBLO

Two and the Pueblo is a portrait of daily life. The people are the heart and soul of the pueblo. As the two artisans make their way in the foreground, I see in them dignity and strength. ✹

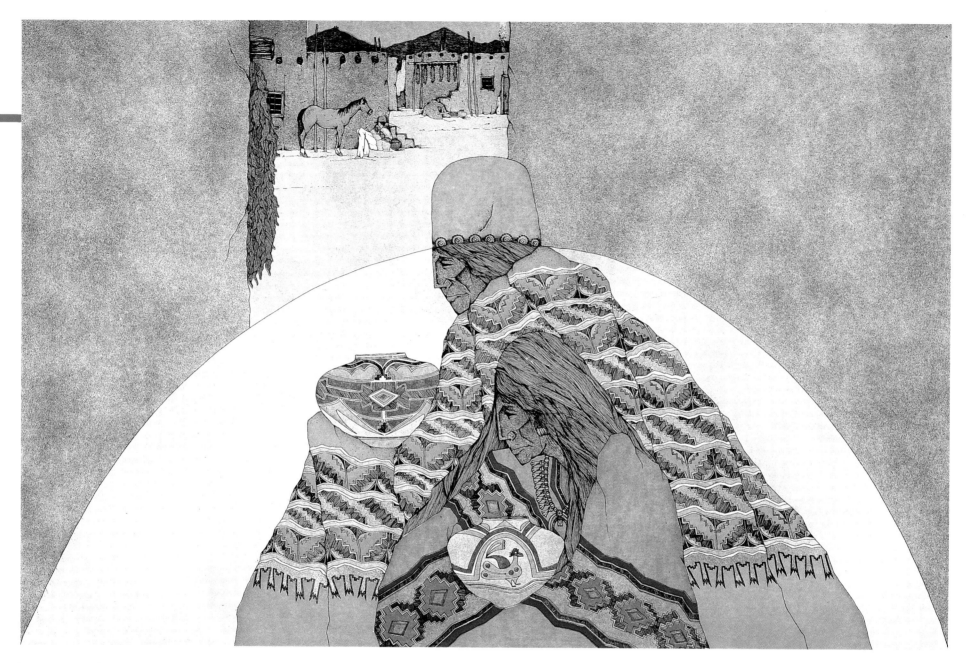

Dos y el Pueblo – 24" x 36" Etching, 1983

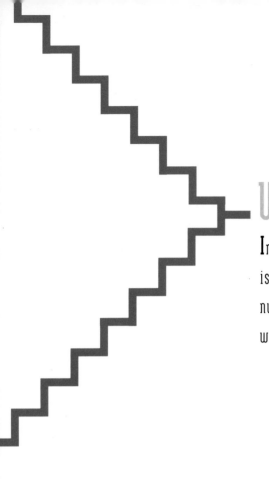

Una Cultura

In this etching, *One Culture,* the most important figure is a child, our seed and our future. His parents protect and nurture him. Symbolism becomes an important element in my work. The motif represents my Mestizo heritage. ✹

Una Cultura — 24" x 18" Etching/Embossed, 1984

ARTESANOS DE SANTA FE

As the artisans travel to a festival, they unite with the splendor of the landscape. Recurring themes are important in my work. Designs representing the land, the animals, and the water are seen in the blankets and pottery. ✷

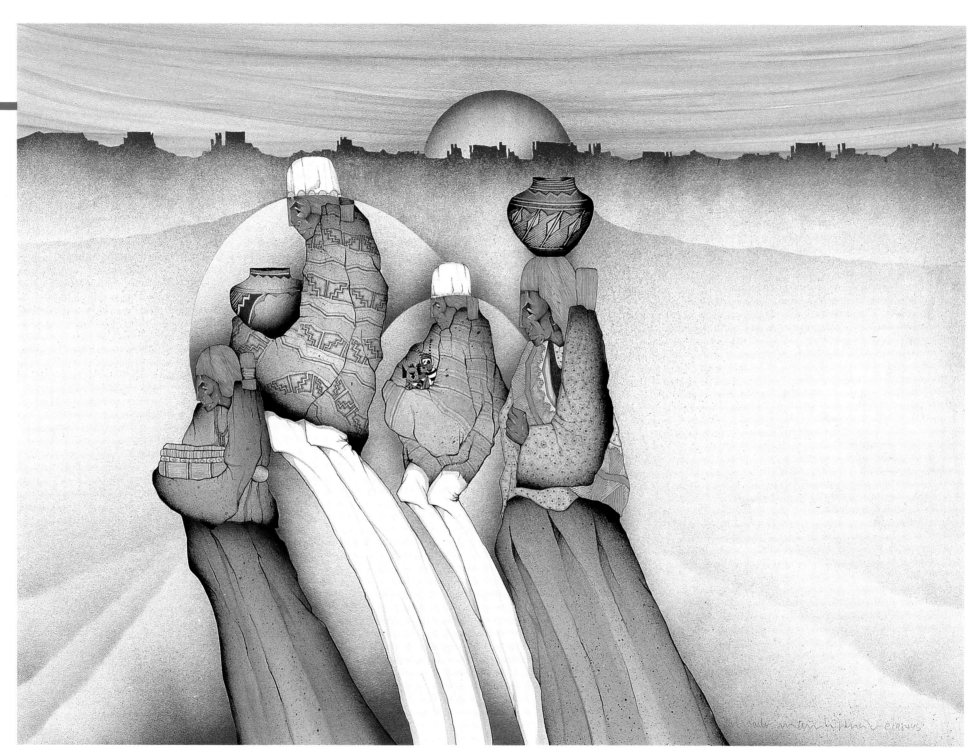

ARTESANOS DE SANTA FE – 30" x 40" MIXED MEDIA PAINTING, 1984

Una Oferta

As we look at *Una Oferta,* our eyes move from all directions to the centrally placed olla. The olla represents an offering. The figures are each making their offering to life as dramatized by the mandala-like sweep of their blankets. The land on the horizon, like wind, seems also to flow centrally. I have tried to say that even though we all do many things, we're all doing the same thing in life as we offer part of ourselves to each other.

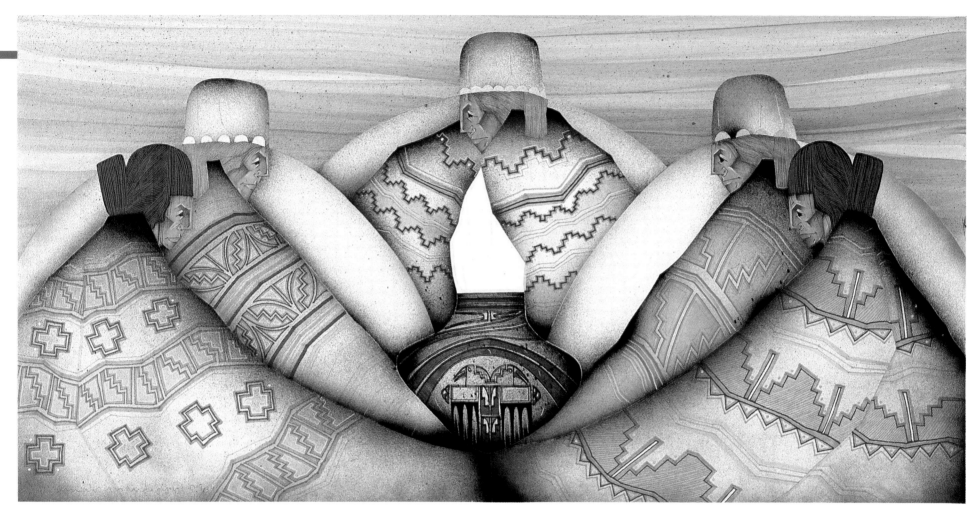

Una Oferta — 24" x 40" Mixed Media Painting, 1984

UN TESORO

In *One Treasure* I have defined the treasure as the art form of the weaver. The designs represented in the weaving and the philosophy behind the designs are meant to show the coming together of the fibers of life. I have a particular love for weaving and collect it with a passion. ✿

UN TESORO — 36" X 20" SERIGRAPH, 1984

ZUNI

Zuni takes my soul back hundreds of years. When I walked through Zuni Pueblo it was like stepping back in time. As I saw the countless structures with soaring ladders reaching to the sky, it evoked a sense of timelessness. The brilliant color of the sky and the artisan with her traditional olla brings me back to the present. ✺

ZUNI – 26" x 34" LITHOGRAPH, 1985

LAS MORADAS

In *Las Moradas*, the majestic purple mountain landscape and the artisans in the foreground are brought together by the pyramid-like pueblo. As the pueblo seems to reach out to the sky, so do we with our dreams and hopes. ✪

LAS MORADAS — 30" x 40" MIXED MEDIA PAINTING, 1985

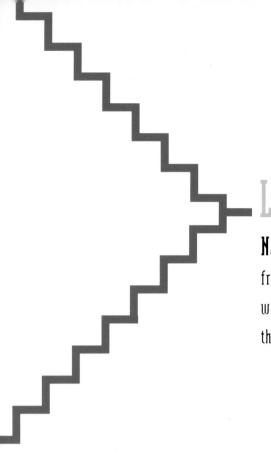

LA PIEDRA

Navajo belief tells us that Spider Woman descended from the top of Spider Rock and taught the Navajo how to weave. *La Piedra, The Rock,* stands in the far background of this pueblo landscape with the weaver today fulfilling this belief. ✪

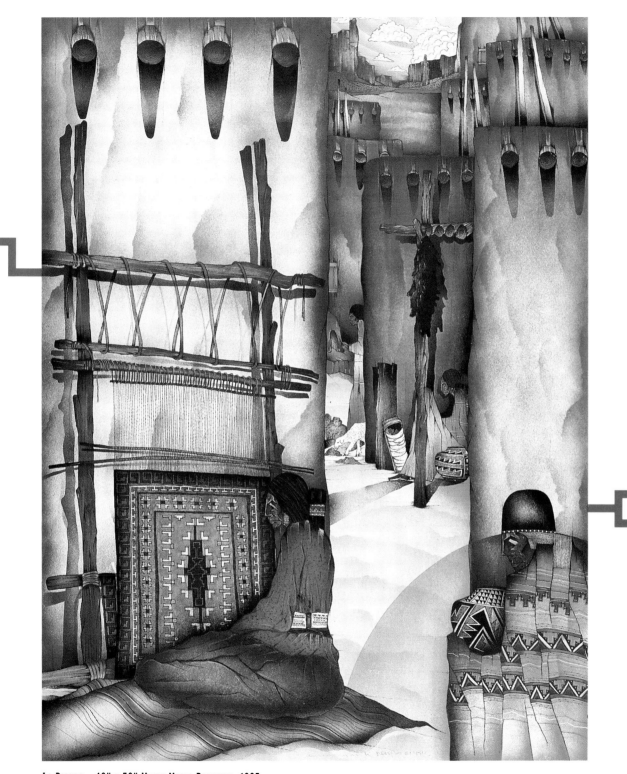

La Piedra — 40" x 30" Mixed Media Painting, 1985

AFTER MARIA: SAN ILDEFONSO

After Maria: San Ildefonso is a portrait of Maria
Martinez, a grand lady. She was considered the matriarch
of San Ildefonso Pueblo and was responsible for bringing the
world's attention to her pueblo people. At times Julian, Maria's
husband, would paint the designs on her pottery. Through the window
we can see the landscape of San Ildefonso Pueblo. Many times I have walked
through their pueblo, many times I have felt their presence. ✿

AFTER MARIA: SAN ILDEFONSO – 30" x 40" MIXED MEDIA PAINTING, 1986

Danza de Noche

A celebration of unity and a coming together of the people is not measured by time. *Danza de Noche* depicts such a celebration. The multiple figures symbolize the strength of my people. We are many in number, but one in soul. ✪

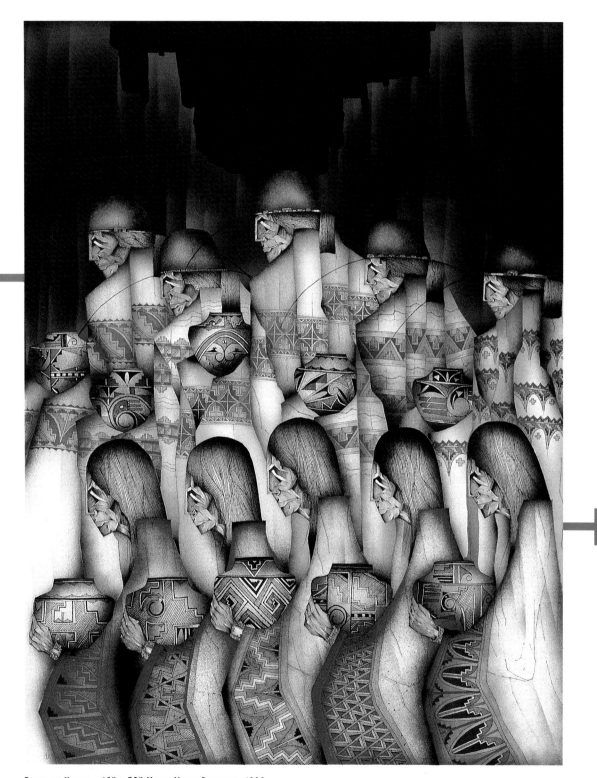

Danza de Noche — 40" x 30" Mixed Media Painting, 1986

CELEBRAMOS

In *We Celebrate* the artisans offer their art to the
world they celebrate. Mother Earth has given them the clay
and the spirit to fulfill that intent, therefore the landscape is
a tribute to her. The black olla represents the coming together of
all people in this celebration. ✿

CELEBRAMOS – 30" x 40" MIXED MEDIA PAINTING, 1986

ARTESANOS ELEGANTES

The Elegant Artisans pays tribute to those individuals who make a difference in giving beauty to this world. As their work is elegant, so they themselves become elegant. The repetitive designs on the blankets and bowls symbolize the many contributions of their efforts to represent their message to us. These designs also represent symbols of the unity of land, water, and animals. ✹

ARTESANOS ELEGANTES — 36" x 22" SERIGRAPH, 1986

ARTESANOS DEL VALLE

In *Artisans of the Valley*, the figures shown below the landscape are truly part of the land. Our culture teaches us the relationship between the people and the land. The land has given us much. The bond between the people and the land must be strong. As a storyteller, I must find a way to express this. ✲

ARTESANOS DEL VALLE – 30" x 40" MIXED MEDIA PAINTING, 1987

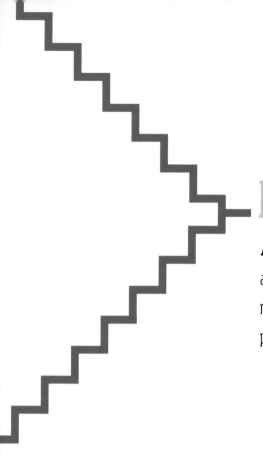

MARIITA

Mariita embodies strength, nobility, perseverance and dignity. These are qualities that characterize my mother, Maria, a colorful individual in her own quiet way. He presence is strong, and just by her presence people react to her. ✺

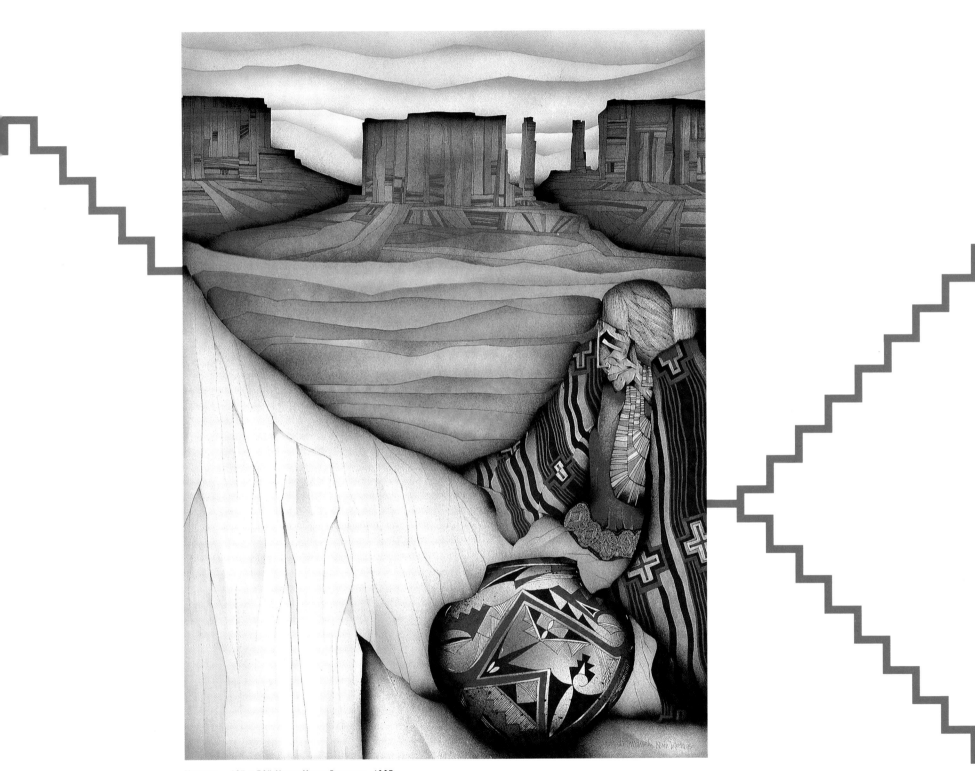

Mariita — 40" x 30" Mixed Media Painting, 1987

La Oferta

In the Mestizo culture, water is an element that gives life. In trying to make this statement, the two figures cradle the olla, representing the people consuming life. The fertile waters flow to the land, giving it and the people life. The water serpent, a mythological pueblo character, protects the waters. As the landscape protects the people, it also becomes part of life's offering. We are one with the elements... water... the land. ✵

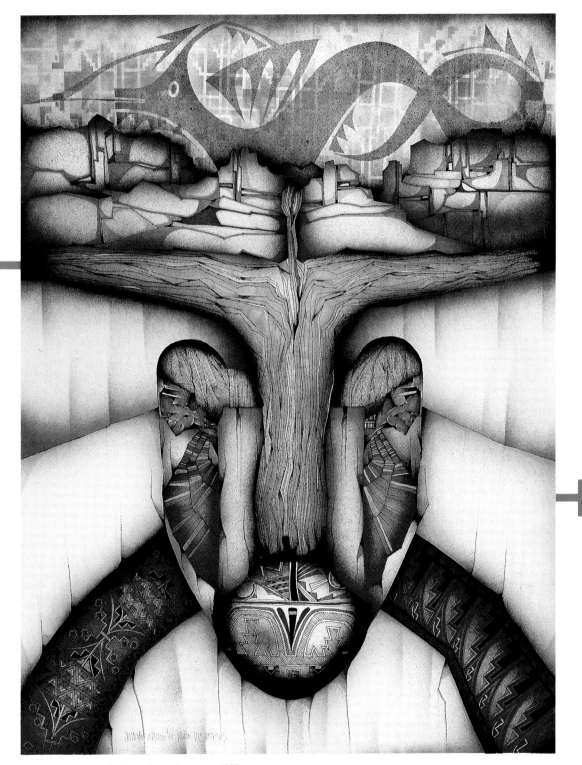

La Oferta — 40" x 30" Mixed Media Painting, 1987

LO NUESTRO

Lo Nuestro is a portrait of our indigenous heritage. We are Mestizo. The circle extending from the figure's hat represents infinity with no beginning or end. The multiple figures represent a landscape. Together they become our roots, our heritage. ✪

LO NUESTRO — 23" X 18" SERIGRAPH, 1987

OLLA DE ACOMA

Through the years I have been fortunate to have made many friends, many of them artists. They come from all over the country, from very special places. One special friend, who was like a grandmother to me, came from the southwestern pueblo of Acoma. Her family took me in as one with them. Her friendship and my admiration for her inspired this particular work of art. ✪

OLLA DE ACOMA – 30" x 18" EMBOSSED ETCHING, 1988

Los Regalos de Lucy

As a further tribute to Lucy Lewis and her pueblo of Acoma, I present this portrait. In her lifetime she touched many people through her art. It is in this painting that I try to say thanks to her for touching my heart with her friendship. I will always be grateful. ✿

LOS REGALOS DE LUCY — 40" x 30" MIXED MEDIA PAINTING, 1988

TEJANITA

As a tribute to all artists of Texas, I painted this image. Born and raised in Texas, *Tejanita* embodies the love and respect I have for my fellow artisans. We have so much to offer to the world with our art that you don't have to create it in Paris or New York, but where your heart is... Texas! ✺

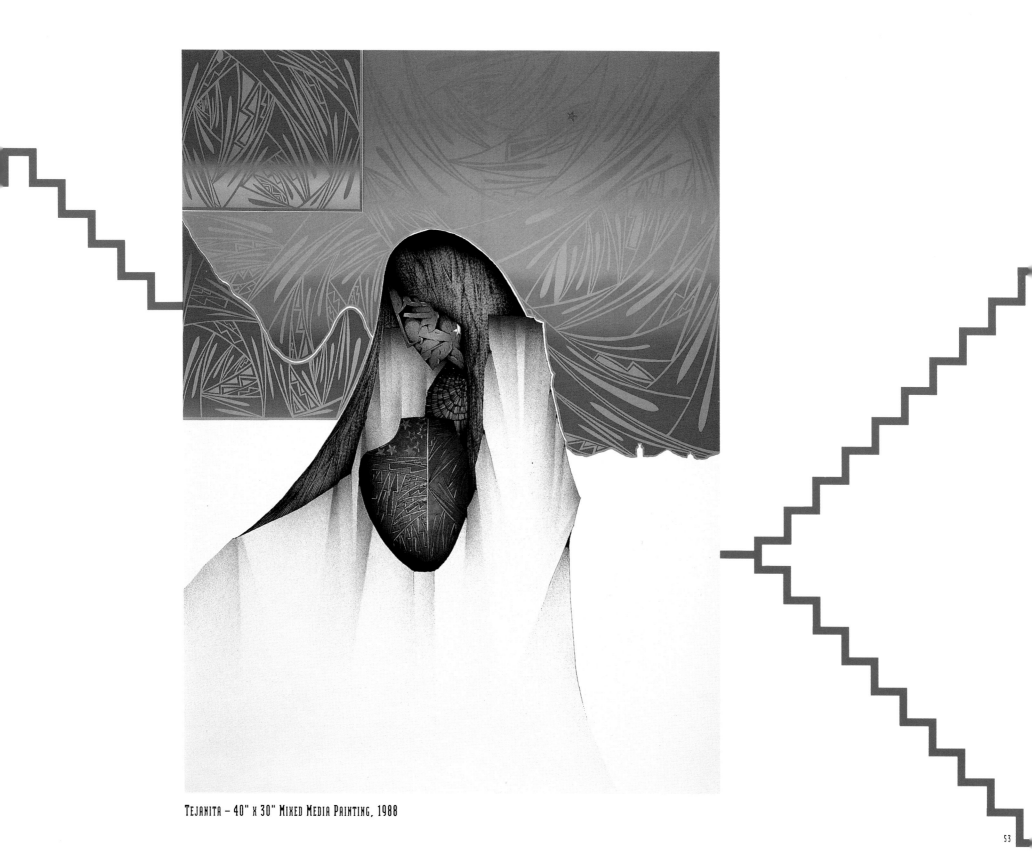

TEJANITA — 40" x 30" MIXED MEDIA PAINTING, 1988

Colcha y Olla

The artisan makes her offering to the land and to the people. She has taken Mother Earth and molded her into a work of art – a work of beauty. She paints designs to pay tribute to life – animal designs, cloud designs, water designs. She gives thanks by kneeling... showing her humility. ✹

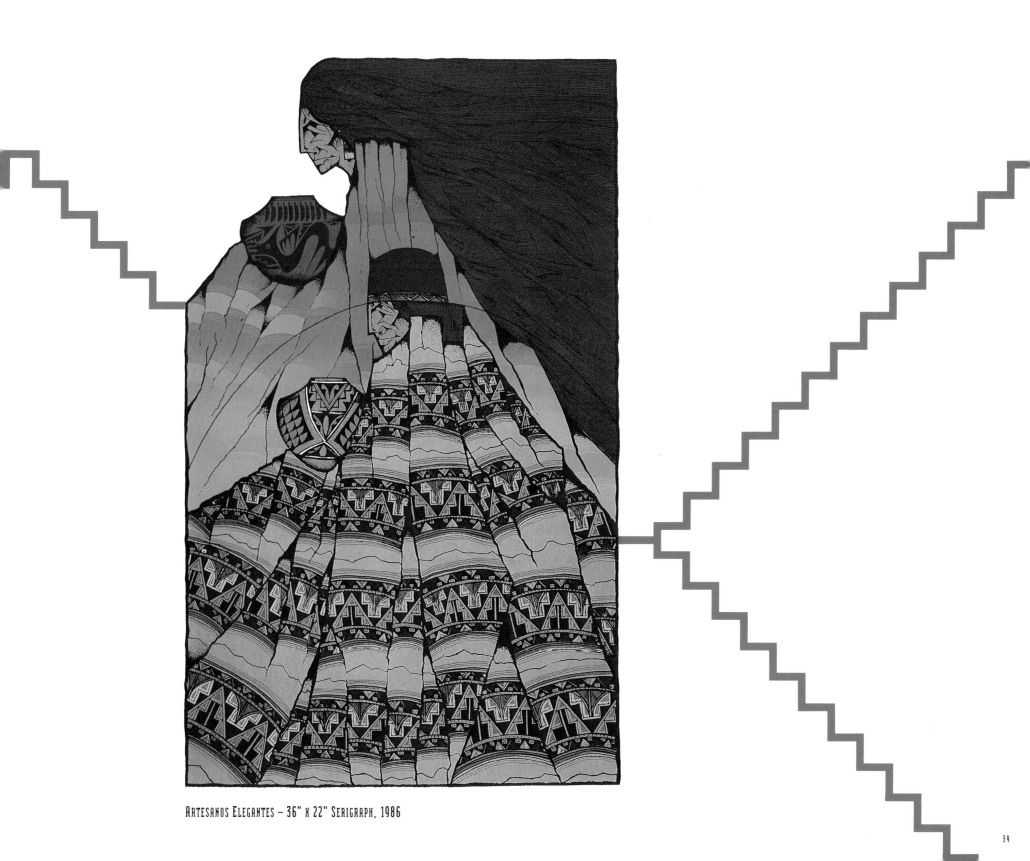

ARTESANOS ELEGANTES – 36" x 22" SERIGRAPH, 1986

Artesanos del Valle

In *Artisans of the Valley,* the figures shown below the landscape are truly part of the land. Our culture teaches us the relationship between the people and the land. The land has given us much. The bond between the people and the land must be strong. As a storyteller, I must find a way to express this. ✺

Artesanos del Valle — 30" x 40" Mixed Media Painting, 1987

MARIITA

Mariita embodies strength, nobility, perseverance and dignity. These are qualities that characterize my mother, Maria, a colorful individual in her own quiet way. He presence is strong, and just by her presence people react to her. ✺

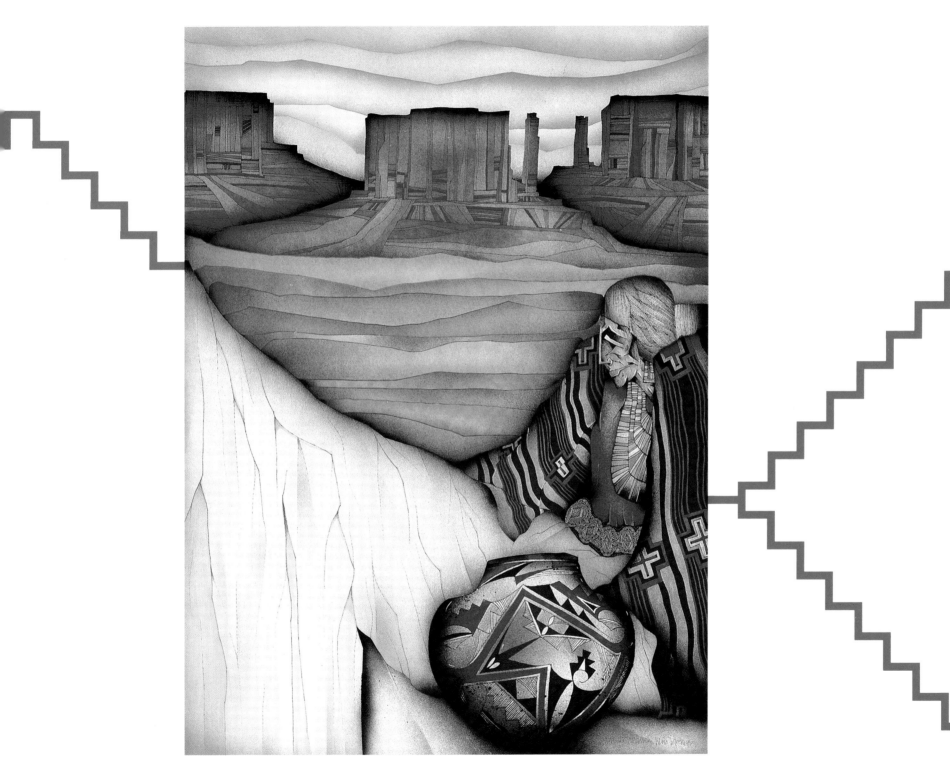

MARIITA – 40" x 30" MIXED MEDIA PAINTING, 1987

La Oferta

In the Mestizo culture, water is an element that gives life. In trying to make this statement, the two figures cradle the olla, representing the people consuming life. The fertile waters flow to the land, giving it and the people life. The water serpent, a mythological pueblo character, protects the waters. As the landscape protects the people, it also becomes part of life's offering. We are one with the elements... water... the land. ✵

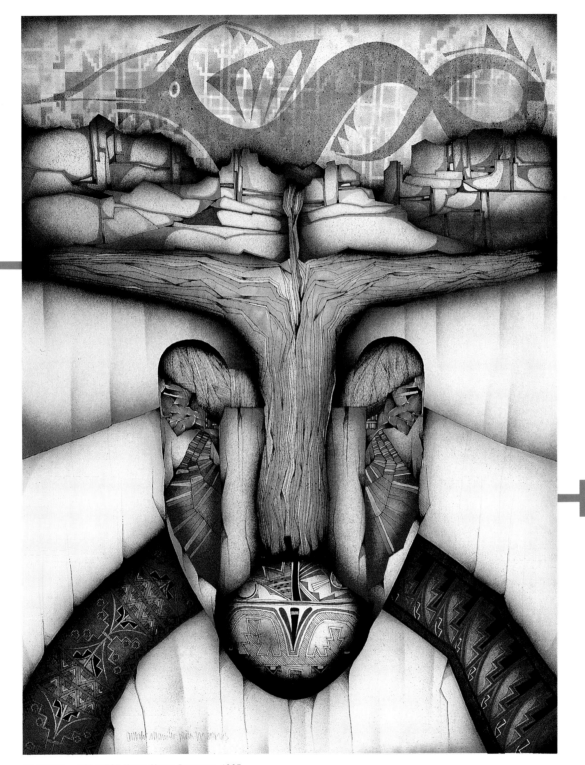

LA OFERTA — 40" x 30" MIXED MEDIA PAINTING, 1987

Lo Nuestro

Lo Nuestro is a portrait of our indigenous heritage.
We are Mestizo. The circle extending from the figure's hat
represents infinity with no beginning or end. The multiple
figures represent a landscape. Together they become our roots,
our heritage. ✪

OLLA DE ACOMA – 30" x 18" EMBOSSED ETCHING, 1988

Los Regalos de Lucy

As a further tribute to Lucy Lewis and her pueblo of Acoma, I present this portrait. In her lifetime she touched many people through her art. It is in this painting that I try to say thanks to her for touching my heart with her friendship. I will always be grateful. ✪

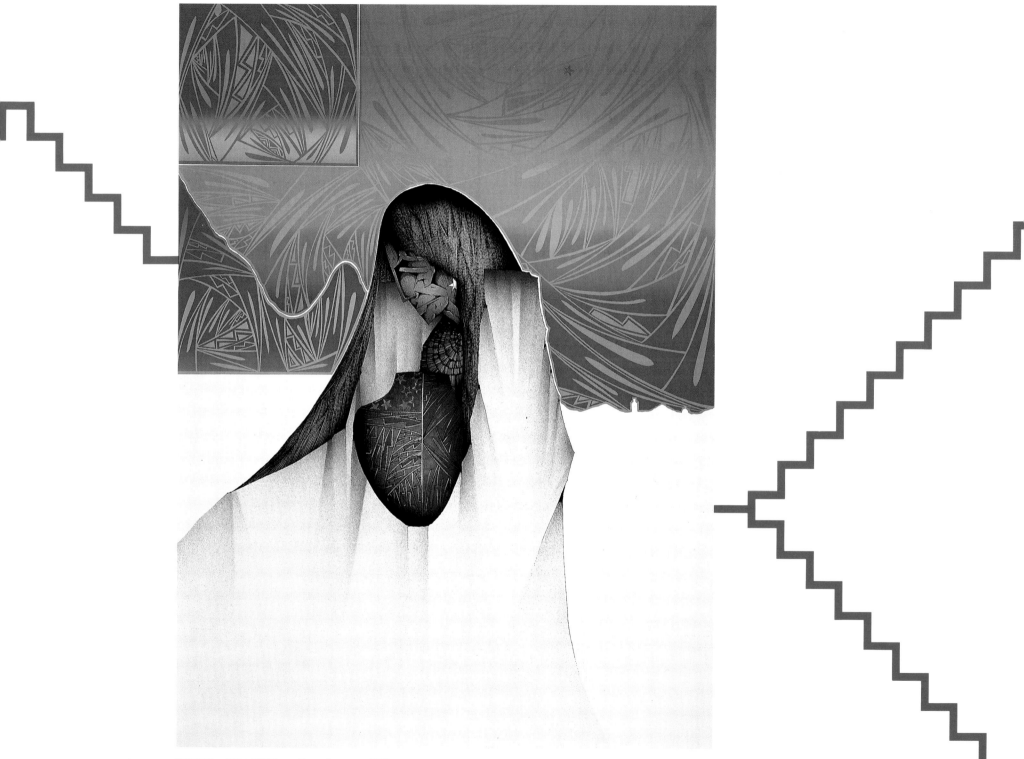

TEJANITA — 40" X 30" MIXED MEDIA PAINTING, 1988

Colcha y Olla

The artisan makes her offering to the land and to the people. She has taken Mother Earth and molded her into a work of art – a work of beauty. She paints designs to pay tribute to life – animal designs, cloud designs, water designs. She gives thanks by kneeling... showing her humility. ✹

COLCHA Y OLLA — 32" x 26" SERIGRAPH, 1988

COLCHA SERIES

As I looked around my home one day I came across a
collection of old Navajo weavings. As I unfolded them,
they felt a hundred years old, they smelled of old. It made me
think of the weaver and her many hours of loving labor it took to
make such a blanket. I asked myself, was it enough to just see them,
feel them, smell them? No – I must paint them, I must draw them. I must
record them in some way. So I did. ✪

COLCHA SERIES — 36" X 24" ETCHING, 1989

La Melodia

The Melody, a romantic representation of life, is a song of love, a song of hope, a song of joy – a song in all of us. The sound of this song is meant to flow through our soul and allow us to share life with one another. ✸

La Melodia — 48" x 72" Acrylic on Canvas, 1989

Los Diez

Five artisans, five ollas, ten years – a portrait of time. So many rewards, so many friends. How can I say what I have shared through time? I feel my spirit flow in all directions and then come together in the end. I paint with that passion with hopes that my images will touch someone. ✺

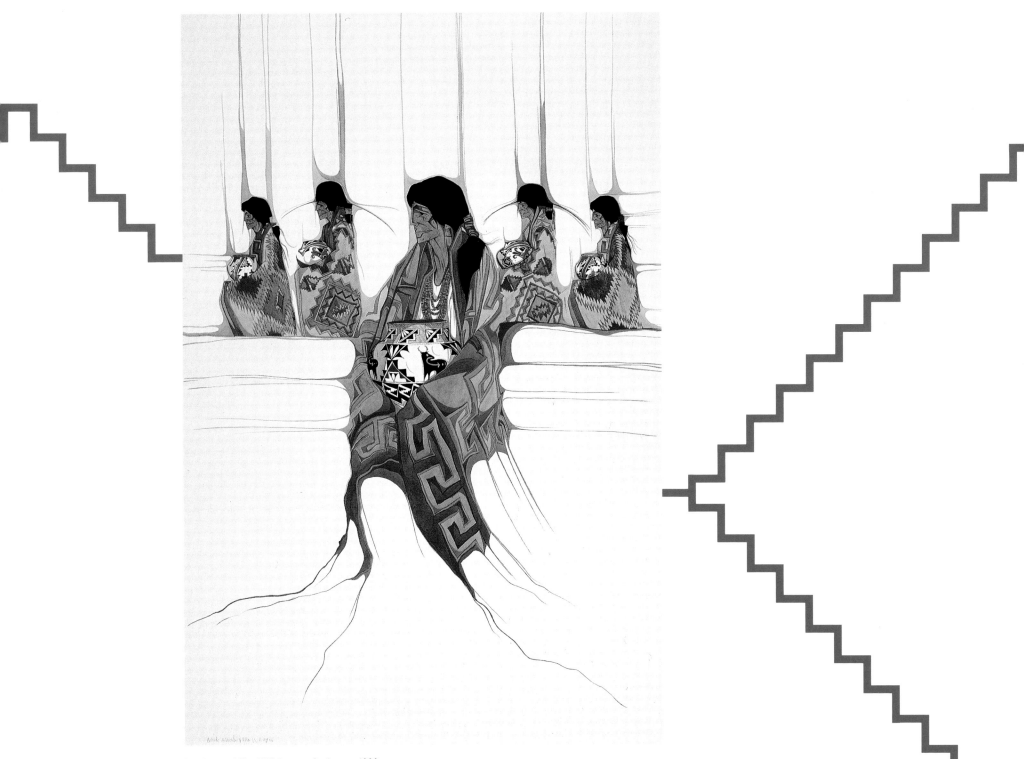

LOS DIEZ – 40" x 30" ACRYLIC ON PAPER, 1989

Kiva y Mujer

In *Woman and Kiva,* she sits in majestic splendor, shimmering in all of her glory. Her elegant wealth is displayed by her worldly possessions. She glances at the distance where the kiva – a ceremonial lodge – stands anchoring the simple landscape. She thinks of a time in her life when things were simple. She ponders the blending of the Christian world and her native traditions. The hard times of living in two worlds is measured by the distance between the figure and the kiva. ✿

KIVA Y MUJER — 38" X 23.25" MIXED MEDIA DRAWING/EMBOSSED, 1989

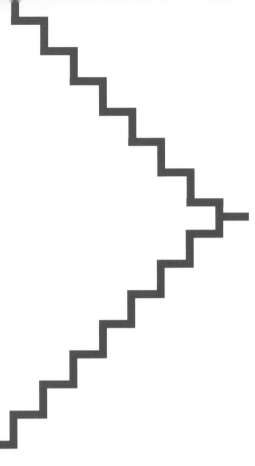

COLORES

Colores means "Many Colors." While life is simple, it is very complex. Where the process of making art is simple, the stories behind the art are complex. While the viewer enjoys the multitude of colors in my work, he may not see the complicated processes. In the end, the beauty of the imagery, the beauty of the colors outlive all intentions. ✺

Colores — 21.5" x 27.5" Serigraph, 1989

LOS ARTESANOS

Los Artesanos is a tribute to all artisans. As artists we
are expected to communicate with our audience, however,
we may not always succeed at this. I believe I am two people.
As a philosopher and storyteller, I try to tell stories about my culture.
On the other hand, I am an artist, a contemporary. As an artist I am also
trying to express artistic philosophies. Sometimes there is a conflict between
both. In time the audiences will understand both of us. ✿

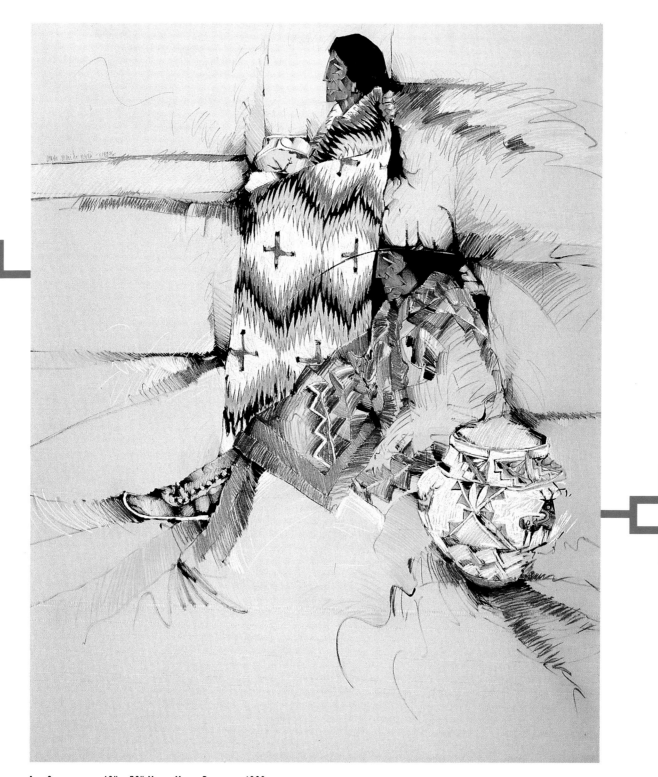

LOS ARTESANOS – 48" x 36" MIXED MEDIA DRAWING, 1989

PATRONES EN COLORES

Patterns of Many Colors is a reflection of life itself.
The figure is interwoven with the designs and colors, which
represent life's complexities. As we try to live in both the white
man's world and our Mestizo world, we are reminded of the struggles
we have overcome. In the midst of all the turmoil we can still appreciate
the good things about life. ✸

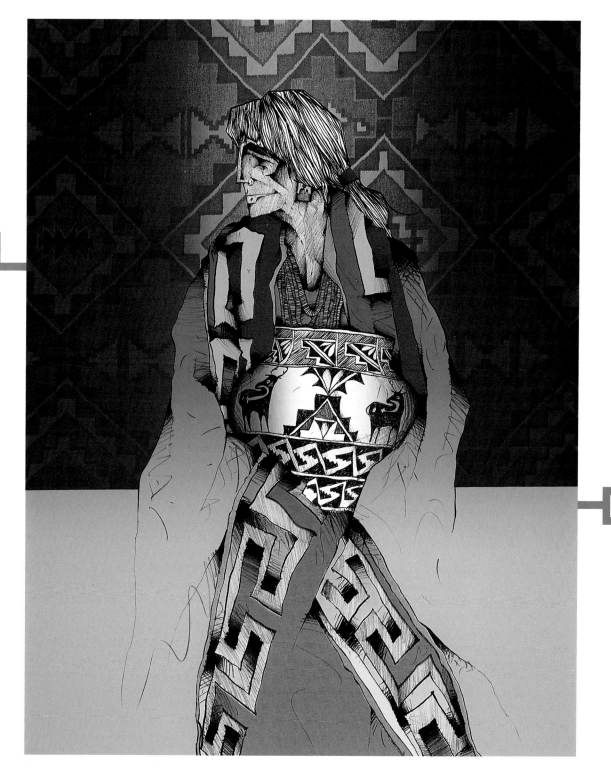

PATRONES EN COLORES — 34" X 26" LITHOGRAPH, 1989

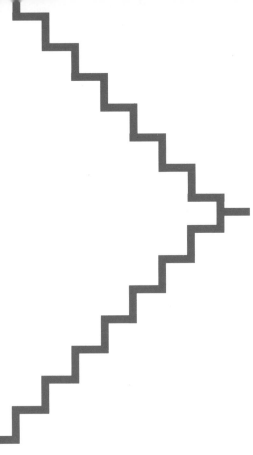

EL CHONGO

El Chongo – The Braid –

What is beauty? Beauty is a woman touching her hair...
looking into the distance asking, Where has time gone? In my
culture the woman is very important. She is the strength of her
people. Most of the time she is portrayed as a hardworking individual.
Sometimes we forget her femininity. Her presence is poetry. With this painting
I try to give thanks for her beauty. ✷

EL CHONGO — 48" x 48" MIXED MEDIA PAINTING, 1990

DOS AL BAILE

Dos al Baile is a dance, a celebration, a coming together in life. As the two dance, life's rhythm flows through them represented by the colors coming from all directions. With each step they become one with each other, making them stronger. They become one. ✪

Dos al Baile – 40" x 60" Transparent Acrylic, 1990

PAJARITO Y VENADO

Pajarito y Venado – A Little Bird and the Deer. One of the beautiful things about our culture is the understanding of those things that give us life. I hope that through my art I will have recorded this philosophy. I hope I will be able to make others understand my culture through my work. ✺

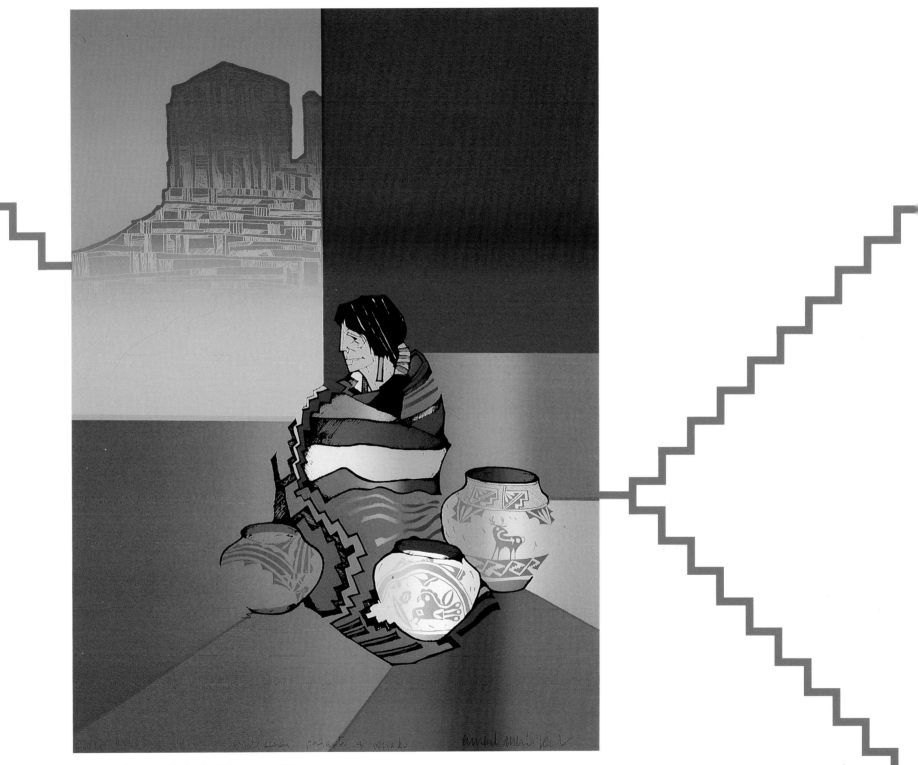

PAJARITO Y VENADO – 24.5" X 17.5" SERIGRAPH, 1990

OLLA ROSA

Olla Rosa is an exploration of my art in a contemporary way. I take what is in my heart and explore those feelings on paper.

My passion for color...

My love for design...

My reason for being alive:

Olla Rosa is a portrait of the artist. ✿

Olla Rosa – 16" x 11" Serigraph, 1990

Cuatro del Valle

Four of the Valley brings to life the human qualities
of the ollas, because they are part of our culture. The
setting is Monument Valley, a special, holy place for the Navajo
peoples, who invited me in as an outsider to share the land. In my
lifetime I will have made thousands of images in many different mediums.
I have been blessed by a higher power who has given me this talent. I look at
things differently than most people. I have an ability to understand things around
me in a different way. I must have a way of making pictures of these things; the people,
the land. How many ways can I paint them? ✸

Cuatro del Valle – 35" x 26" Serigraph, 1990

Maiz y Metate

To our people, corn is life. I remember my grandmother grinding the corn. Maize became nourishment for her family, a way of life, even life itself. ✲

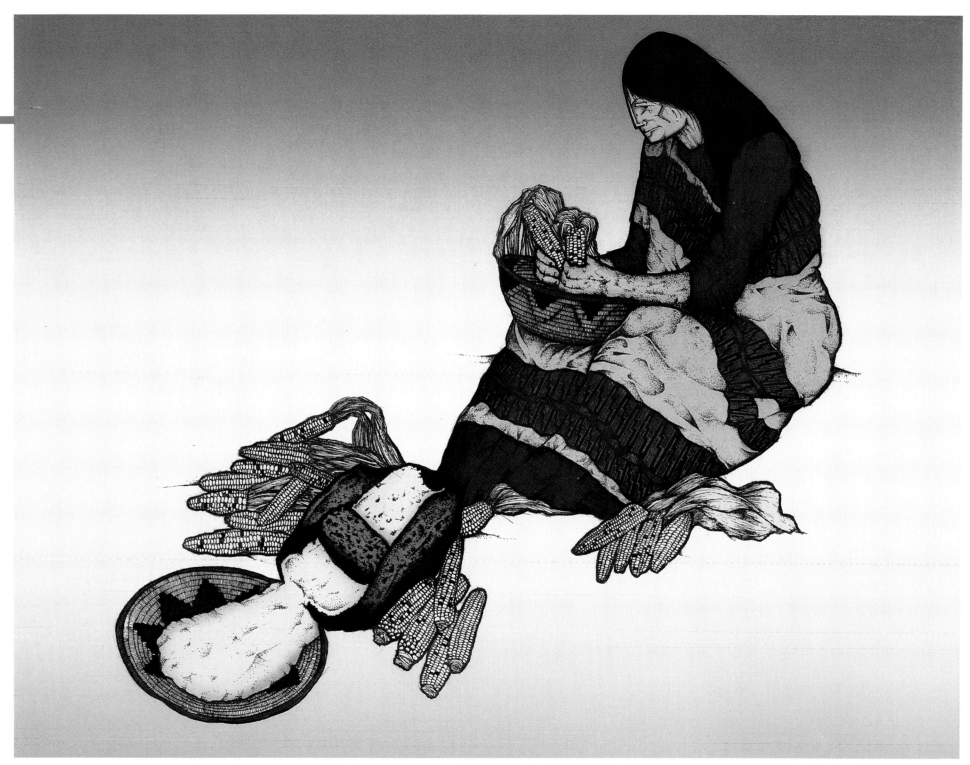

Maiz y Metate — 17" x 22.5" Etching, 1991

CELEBRAMOS

Celebramos – We Celebrate

As they look in opposite directions, the figures become one.
Through their creations, the artisans share with us the beauty
of life as depicted by the designs on the ollas. Regardless of the
different types of designs, each design represents the same philosophy –
that which has to do with life. Because of that they become recurring themes
in my work. When a creation is made, there is a celebration. ✺

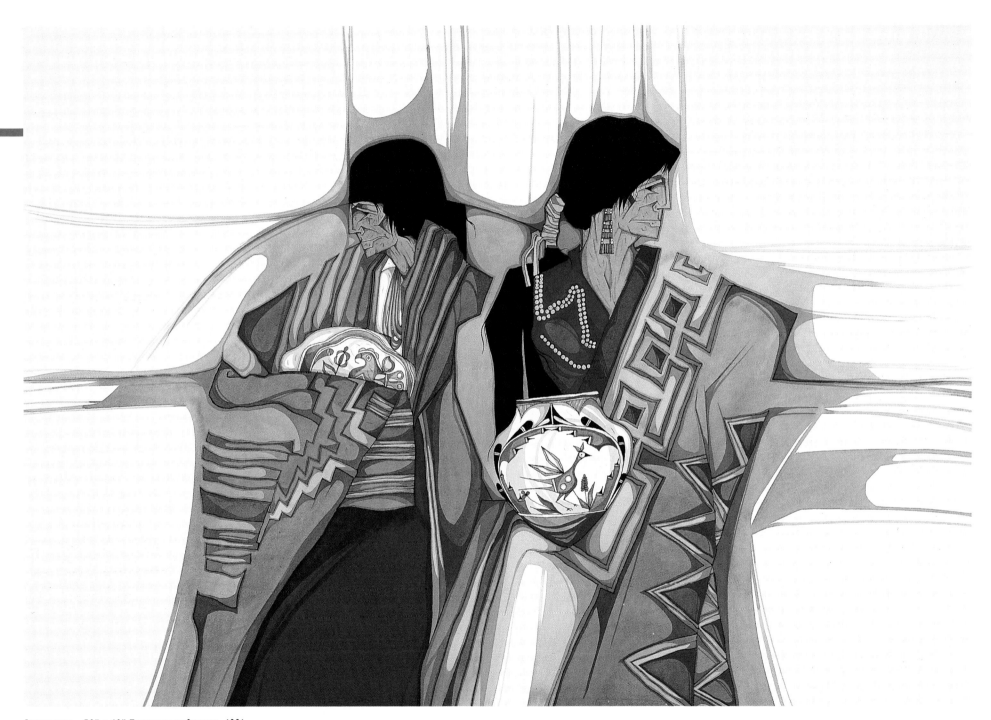

CELEBRAMOS — 30" x 40" TRANSPARENT ACRYLIC, 1991

Dos Hermanitas

Two Sisters – and yet one. Two sisters with a kindred spirit and an abstract background that lets them be any two sisters on earth. ✸

Dos Hermanitas — 20" x 13" Serigraph, 1991

Melodia de Oro

A *Melody in Gold* –

As much as I love to show our culture through images of land and water and animals, sometimes it's also an ethereal celebration of music.

    a melody of hope

    a melody of love

    a melody of happiness

    a melody that unites us in life as one –

    a melody in gold. ✺

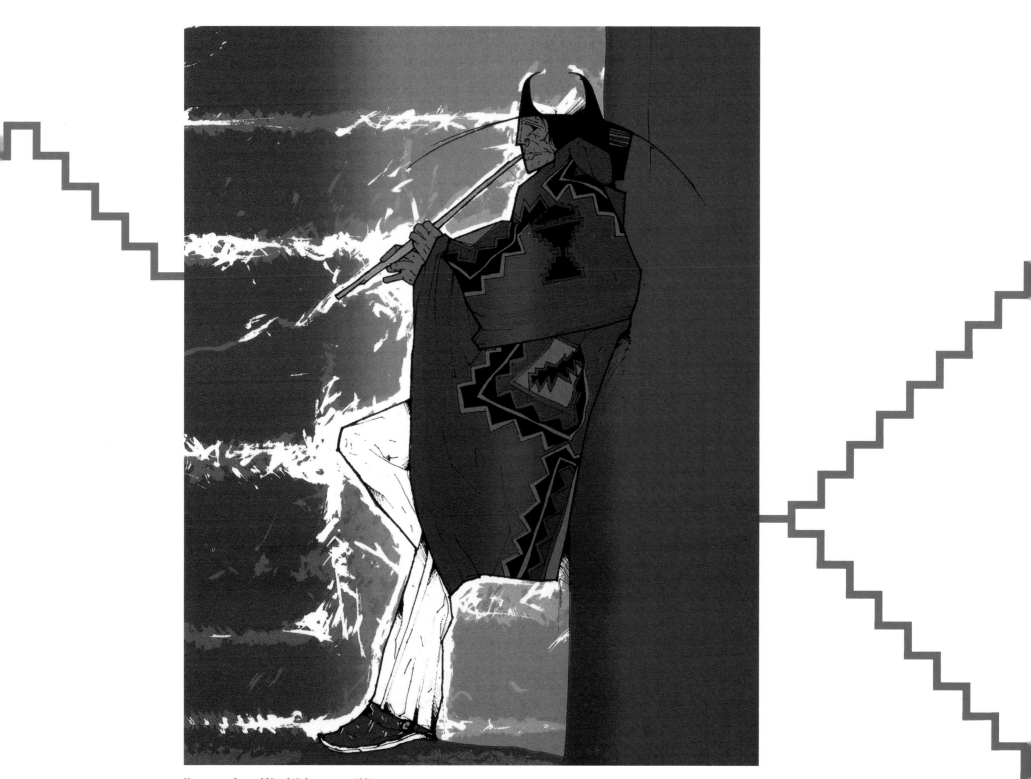

MELODIA DE ORO – 26" X 21" SERIGRAPH, 1991

SANTO DOMINGO

Santo Domingo... one of the many Rio Grande pueblos in
the Southwest. The pueblo people have become an important
part of my life. The many influences, like beliefs and religion,
are similar to that of the Mestizo culture. I remember first being
introduced to a pueblo elder... his name was Incarnacion Peña. He was an
artist. We first became friends. Later I became his adopted grandson. ✦

Santo Domingo – 16" x 15" Lino-Serigraph, 1991

ROJA

One in Red. Tradition is so important in our culture. One may be removed from his people, but as long as he remembers where he came from, he will always be close to them. Tradition teaches us to be strong, to be proud. Sometimes I try to make statements about such things. Sometimes by using abstract images I will say this. ✿

Roja — 13.5" x 11" Lino-Serigraph, 1991

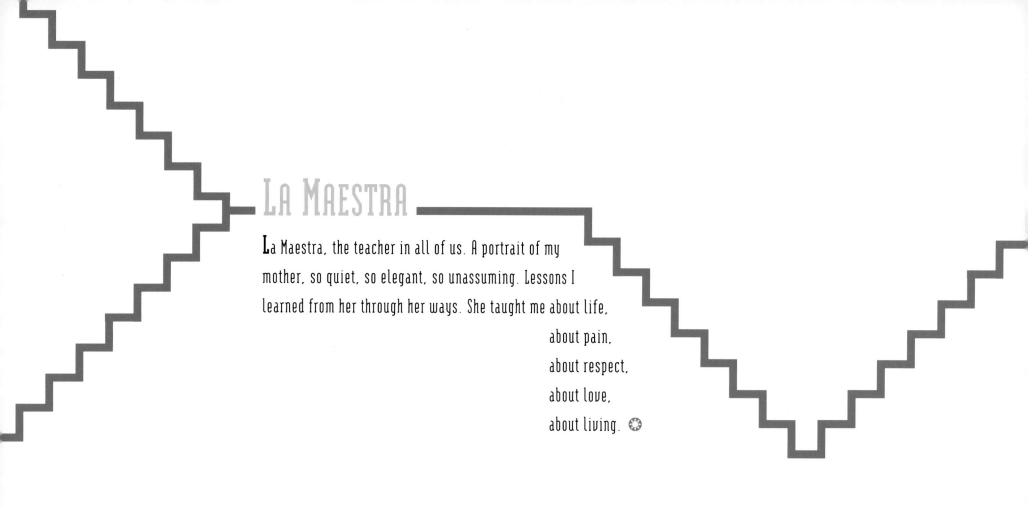

La Maestra

La Maestra, the teacher in all of us. A portrait of my
mother, so quiet, so elegant, so unassuming. Lessons I
learned from her through her ways. She taught me about life,

about pain,

about respect,

about love,

about living.

La Maestra — 24" x 18" Monotype, 1992

Mujer, Bisonte y Acoma con Valle

Woman, Bison and Acoma speaks about the very essence of my work. As I take time to put the past few years in perspective, I realize how fortunate I am to be able to do one of the most important things in my life... my artwork. Also, I am made aware of the many people who have influenced and guided me along the way. I hope that through my work I have paid tribute to them. I hope my work will have told the story of the Mestizo people to everyone, everywhere. ✪

Mujer, Bisonte y Acoma con Valle – 42" x 32" Monotype, 1993

amado maurilio peña Jr.